HELLF

Shai Kara

ACKNOWLEDGEMENTS

I want to start by thanking my wonderful husband, Matthew Hunt, and my sister, Sophia Kara, for supporting me in writing this book. From listening to me recite my poems and providing feedback, to editing multiple drafts of this book, to helping me design a cover page, I truly could not have finished this book without you.

I also wish to thank my parents for supporting me in all things and my late grandmother for inspiring me to be the woman I am today.

This is not the book you open
When you want to feel better,
When you need reassurance and comfort.

This is not for you
If you cower at the truth,
If you desire to live each day
With your eyes open but not seeing,
Hearing but not listening.

This is not what you read
When you need a pick-me-up.
It is what you read
When you are finally comfortable
Acknowledging the bitterness
Of the world you live in
While still seeing the beauty
In all things painful.

This is raw.
This is unapologetic.
This is true.

These are @storiesbyshai

CONTENTS

SPARKS

There is pain on the pages you never read,
Ink from a pen that bled
All the hurt into words when you left.
There are tears from the sleepless nights
When writing helped drown out the cries
And the unbearable fights
That kept me awake.

There is hurt from the bite marks on my chest
When lies ate me alive
And drowned out the rest
Of the life I could have led.

Even if I let you see the pages in my book,
I doubt you could read between the lines,
See the pain behind the smiles,
The tears behind the laughs,
The love behind the hate,
The anguish in my fate.

There is pain on the pages that you will never read.

There you stand
At the edge of a bed,
So careful not to cry
But the hurt eats you up inside
So you decide to share it with her.
Your little girl carries it gladly,
Wears it like armour
So no bullets can touch her.
The pain her heart carries
Has become her protector.

I sincerely hope it made your heart lighter
When you gave your pain to her.

Our days turned to night
Without a warning sign.
Without a kiss goodbye,
The sun turned off its light,
And it has been dark ever since.

- An empty home

Your pain is my prison.
I feel like I'm locked in a cage,
Kicked in my stomach
Every time you scream,
I cry it out in rage.
How much can a young heart take
When it hurts to stay awake?

I see you cry, and you see me.
You force a smile
So I smile back,
Hoping it will help
But you turn away
Before I can see another tear
Roll down your face.

It's a disgrace to divorce, you say.
But what if it would take the pain away?
I will stand by your side,
Hold your hand in mine;
We will make it out okay.

But you choose to stay.

Your pain is my prison
But that's okay —
I will hold your hand, anyway.

Once upon a time,
When I was a little girl,
I was gifted a beautiful doll.
I cared for her very much,
Played with her every day.
I bathed her, washed her hair, changed her clothes.
She slept in my bed so she would not feel lonely.
I brought her along to birthday parties,
Fed her my share of cake and candy.
I thought she would be with me forever.

But as time passed,
Her hair started falling out,
Her clothes browned.
I tried so hard to keep her beautiful
That her beauty faded.

I cried and I cried.
I had to say goodbye,
Give her an unwanted burial.
When I was a little girl,
I wondered for the first time,
How is it that we can destroy what we love
By giving too much love?

- Love is a paradox

You change colours like the weather
And today, there is a storm.

I can't speak the words aloud
Without knowing what truly happened
And a part of what happened
Was your intention.
So did you know what you were doing?
Did you know it was wrong,
When you preyed on someone so young?
Or were you, too, a victim all along,
Just continuing the cycle of what happened to you?

- The cycle of abuse

The sun may rise in paradise
But trust me, it's still dark.
The light may shine and fill the room
But this house is as cold as your heart.

Summer comes and although it's hot,
The ice our words create
Leave no space for hope or love;
There's no room to keep our faith.

They say, if you just believe in God,
Nothing will go wrong
But before you think to say the same,
Try calling out God's name.

As I waited for a response, an answer,
I realized that blind belief
Is far more difficult than hate.

The truth is,
I am made of remorse, tears, and hopelessness.
I am merely the by-product of a broken marriage,
A reminder of all that could have been
But was not,

Simply because I was born

New questions every day.
New worries I'm not willing to state
Aloud
Because my thoughts are already too loud.
They go from him
To her,
To love,
To us,
To needing,
To wanting,
To bleeding,
To leaving.
Then those thoughts slip
And there is anxiety
About what,
Where,
When,
Why,
How —
Was I wrong?
I can't remember what I was thinking about.
I tell myself to convince myself,
It's just a thought; It'll go away,
So I let it stay.
It's torture
But I let the thought stay.

- *This* is OCD

You were my best friend
And my worst enemy
All the same.

- Letters to my past self

Shai Kara // Hellfire

How do you know that you're okay
When you've never known what it feels like?
How do you know it's a good day
When all days feel alike?

You tell me I am safe,
But is it safe in a cage?
You tell me it's okay,
That you'll take care of me.

You hold me tight and kiss me nice
And I pretend it makes me feel loved.
You look in my eyes and I try to smile,
But my lips — they just tell lies.

And all this time,
I can't help but wonder,
Why does love feel like thunder?

14

Broken hands
And treasured eyes.
Rest assured,
His words are lies,
Telling you
What you need to hear,
Erasing gut feelings
And inner fears.

Lustful lips
And heavy cries.
Forever comes
Where peace will die.
Eternities pass
But regrets remain.
Love is true
But happiness is feigned.

- Prison is a feeling, not a place

It's like I'm trapped in a dark room
I can't escape from,
Thinking thoughts
I can't move on from.
All I see in this darkness is your face,
The memories we made.
That last memory —
I knew that was it.
I felt it inside me,
As if it were a part of me,
Just like I felt you inside me,
Breaking me in.
Something told me to accept it, to face it,
Except I told that something *no*.
I told that feeling to go,
But you went away too.
I wish I could say, *I should have known*
But I knew.
Still, I chose to believe in you.

You asked me when I would let it all go
And I whispered faintly,
The day I stop believing in love.

I love you too much to let it go.

There is a difference between
Trying to convince me that you love me
And truly loving me.

One is selfish; the other is *selfless*.

You say you won't leave again
But how can I even forgive you
For the last time you left
If your absence is the reason
I am no longer the woman you once loved.

- I miss her more than you do

When we argue and I hold in my tears, is that happiness? When I have the strength to pull myself together and move on, is that happiness? Is happiness having half of what you've always wanted in the present, because the past is too horrible to contain, too loud to let go of? Is happiness in the inability to feel love completely because love slipped away the first time? Is it in the attempt to appreciate a moment even when all you can see is hurt in your lover's eyes? Is happiness pretending that it is okay, telling them that it's okay, telling yourself that it's okay, when it's not and never will be?

Or is happiness when you genuinely forget all the wrong and smile without thinking? When your brain is empty of thoughts for one moment and nothing in the world really matters except for what you feel in your heart? When you don't even remember whether something was funny, sweet, or clever? When without a chance to think of what was said, you let out a laugh and it shocks you right to your core, and you wonder, is happiness trying to find its way out? Have you trapped it within you, packed it in so tightly that it sneaks out like air leaving a room through a crack in the window?

Is happiness what could be, what should be, what never will be? Or is happiness what *actually is*?

Does this 'happiness' even exist?

You can have everything you have ever dreamed of and still be unhappy.

- *The hard truth*

It was not easy to walk away from someone
Who embodied home,
With the smell of cigarette smoke
And sweet cologne.

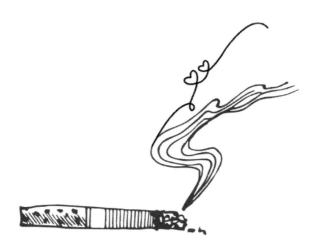

Your hesitation spoke volumes.
Although your words were empty,
Those few seconds of silence
Gave me the answers I needed
To finally leave.

- Silence screams

I should be thankful that you set me free
But this bird can't help but sit in an open cage,
Not knowing how to use her wings
And too afraid to try.

- Learned helplessness

What is love to you, they ask?
And I can only share what I have seen,
So I tell them —

Love is when he promises forever
But only means it for one night.
Love is when he leaves the next day
And forgets to say goodbye.

Love is the silent treatment
That two lovers share,
Passive aggressive remarks,
Purposely displaying a lack of care.
It is when they recruit a middleman
To relay messages between them two
While each silently hopes
The sorrowful letters will end soon.

Love is white lies
And the passion they bring,
The gaslighting, the wondering.
Love is a promise ring
That I wear on my middle finger,
The vows that I keep
When deep in my heart,
I know I should leave.

Love is the anxiety
That comes from believing
And as day turns to night,
Ends with grieving.

Love is loss.

You were the candle
That had lit my way,
Illuminated my path
For decades.

How could I have known
The path you lit
Was leading me
To a world of isolation?
How did your light
Lead me into darkness?

I can hardly explain how it felt
When you ripped me apart,
Tore off my thick skin,
Stomped on my heart.

Your weapons were words,
The most hurtful kind.
They weren't curses or insults;
They were lies.

You made me believe things
That weren't true,
Doubt my own memories
Before I thought to doubt you.

When I said that you were wrong,
Perhaps lying or forgetting,
You looked at me like
I was crazy, overreacting.

Guilting me into thinking
I was mistaken and petty,
Caused me to go to bed
Questioning my own reality.

I would constantly wonder
If I was mentally unstable,
Would I die this way
Or learn to see false from real?

My memories changed
As I trusted your experience.
I tried to scrub myself of
What I thought was delirium.

. . .

...

In you, I finally believed,
Although it took time;
I decided to make you
My eyes, ears, and guide.

Sometime later,
The truth knocked on our door.
We had no choice but to answer it;
There was no hiding anymore.

I can still remember
The way your face changed in front of me.
I'll never forget
That nightmare of a memory.

It soon become clear
There was nothing wrong with me.
I was right all along,
But still I wondered, *was I really?*

The doubt would kill me,
Rip my brain to pieces
And from this trauma,
There was no healing.

I can hardly explain how it felt,
To be programmed to doubt myself.
My tears, cuts, and bruises
Were a cry for help,
That no one heard.

...

...

Perhaps I could have shouted louder,
But I thought I was in the wrong.
You don't realize your weakness
When you think you're being strong.

I still can't believe there was a time
You convinced me to believe in lies.
Little did I know back then
That it was all a *gaslight*.

It was as though there were knives in my stomach
Trying to fight their way out
And my insides were bleeding
But I couldn't even shout.

- Helplessness

If I was given a brick to hold
For every time you lied to me,
I would no longer be.

Your lies don't just hurt —
They crush me.

I remember when you looked at me
And told me I was born to be a therapist,
When you told me I would be great
At helping those in pain.

My dream from when I was a little girl
Was to heal the broken souls,
Help them find joy in the world,
Feel peace when their stories were told.

But I guess what you said was untrue
Because no dreams can come true
When you're deceived and left broken,
Unsure of how to move forward.

You looked me in the eyes
And spoke nothing but lies.
It took me time to discover the truth
But when I did, I was paralyzed.

I did try to move on, push forward,
And focus on what I 'needed'
But maybe my mind changed
When my life was recreated.

And just like that,
Goodbye to the old me, I said,
I guess my dreams are dead.

I started drinking every night.
Three drinks in and I felt alright.
Soon enough, drinks were all I needed
To cope with the demons inside.

...

…
When I thought of the old me,
All the dreams of who I could be,
I told myself, *maybe one day*
But for now, I'll drink my dreams away.

When I discovered the truth,
My whole life changed.
My world collapsed –
No sleep, no break.
I couldn't tell
Imagination from reality.
All that I needed
Was some stability.

But instead of providing me
With solid ground,
Building a path
For me to walk along,
You dug a hole so deep,
I couldn't stop falling through,
And when I finally caught a rope,
I was too weak to run from you.

You could have thrown
Your lies into a grave,
Covered them with dirt
Or burned the remains.
You could have freed me
From the pain and the hurt
And finally allowed
The truth to emerge.

But you could not do it;
It was too manly to do.
That's when I realized
There was no man in you.

- You chose to *bury me* instead

When you're being abused,
You're the prisoner of your abuser.
When the abuse stops,
You're a prisoner to your mind.

- *Trauma*

I hate you more than I have hated anyone
For doing to me what you did,
But I stay because I care
And I hate because I hurt.
Sometimes, in moments, I love you.
In others, I just don't want to lose you
And deal with the grief of being alone.

I don't stay because I need you,
But there are moments in which I want you,
When you make kind gestures and comfort me —
But when you disregard me, I resent you
For all the horrible things you've done to me
And how you made me into the monster
I never imagined I would be.

But most of the time, I feel confused
Because loving and hating you
Have begun to feel so alike —
Like misery with red roses on the side,
A beautiful home, vodka on ice,
In the midst of a storm —
And I cannot decipher the feelings anymore.

The hate has become so strong,
There is no space for love
Left in our home.

- Dysfunction

He groomed me,
Told me what I wanted to hear.
Compliment after compliment,
Lies upon lies,
Insults upon insults
Shaped me into the broken person I was
Trusting no one but him.

I followed a daily routine
Of waking up feeling empty,
Filling the void with breakfast,
Laughing at lunch,
Crying at dinner,
Agonizing,
Then apologizing.

I was skilfully manipulated
Into becoming his masterpiece
And in the process,
I was stripped
Of all the beautiful pieces of me.

- The 'art' of abuse

Shai Kara // Hellfire

Without trust,
We have nothing.

And I am done
Sitting around in this nothingness
That we call a relationship.

I am through
Withholding my feelings from you.

Without trust, truth, and honesty,
We honestly
Have nothing.

So if you have lied all along,
Then all along
We must have been nothing.

- An empty relationship

I laughed so hard
Because it was hysterical
How someone who made me so happy
Could make me so miserable.

A flood of adrenaline and cortisol,
Followed by a rush of serotonin.
The taste of rotten peaches
And beautiful sunsets.
Like a magical kiss
And a bite on the lips,
Crying out in pain,
Making love, then disdain.
Like promises of rainbows,
Shadowed by lightning storms.
Love and comfort,
Living for no purpose,
Feeling warm after a win,
Icicles growing on bare skin.

Listening to hard rock,
No radio to shut off,
Dancing and twirling,
Without a thought of stopping.
Like saying hello and goodbye,
All at the same time,
Cuts and bruises,
Helping hands and Band-Aids.
The smell of hospitals,
Feelings of stomach pain,
The fresh smell of rain.
Buried alive in a coffin,
Beautifully tucked in,
Waiting for an out,
Unable to shout,
So instead, we sing.

Instead, we sing.

- *The trauma bond*

I fell in love with someone else,
The person you pretended to be.
The man I loved passed away
And with him, me.
The love I felt was built over time,
The more you conformed to my expectations,
The harder you tried.

But in the end, it was all a lie.
The man I loved died.

You said, *what's yours is mine*
And what's mine is yours,
But the trauma is mine
And the lies were yours.

It's funny to think
There was once a time
When running away
Was running towards you —
And when I landed in your arms,
You would give me a hug,
Carefully embrace me
With lies and love.

But it was my fault
What you did and didn't do
Because instead of walking away,
I chose to fall for you.
It was my fault
The concrete caught my body,
Leaving blood and cuts
That I let you mend
When deep down I knew,

You cannot be healed
      By the hands that hurt you.

Now, when I look in the mirror,
All I can see
Are scars on my back
From the times I let you stab me.

- Self-blame

How did I end up like this?
So helpless,
So loveless,
Just wanting someone
To come close,
But I don't let them;
I throw threats at them
So they stay away.
What kind of a life is this
When your favourite dream is sleeping
And your worst nightmare
Is what you do every day:
Breathe

You tell me you love me
While you think of someone else.
When you touch my body,
I, too, long for someone else,
Someone clean
Because your touch feels dirty.
Your lies hurt me.
Then later,
They haunt me.

- Empty love

As you kissed my lips,
I thought of his.
As your green eyes
Looked me up and down,
I pictured them being brown,
Like his skin —
That beautiful sun-kissed skin.
I got lost in his eyes —
Those chilling eyes
That looked into mine
And made love to my soul.

- The worst kind of cheating

Your body is a graveyard
For my darkest sins —
A place of transcendence,
Yet a fall from grace.

Our love feels like undying pain.
Although the worst has passed,
It has left a permanent scar on my heart
That weighs as heavy as a rock.
I feel like my lungs will soon collapse
From the tears I have swallowed the wrong way,
Like every part of me might simply shatter
To a point where it is impossible
To piece this love back together.

Our love feels
        Irreparable.

There is no use in trying to reconcile
The lows with the highs
When my love language is mistrust
And yours has always been white lies.

- Incompatibilities

I can't place blame on anyone else.
This responsibility is a weight
I alone will carry
Because truth be told,
I broke my own heart by staying
When deep down I knew
The right decision was leaving.

I pretended comfort was love
   and wound up with neither.

We had the chance to grow together
But instead, we grew apart

Now we are both left to find a way
To move forward with a broken heart.

In a relationship,
Compassion is the fuel
That keeps us going,
Lies are the leeches
That suck the joy out of us,
But it is resentment
That slowly kills us.

Resentment is the poison.

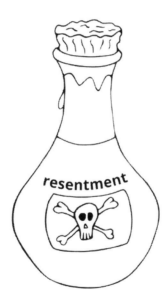

Shai Kara // Hellfire

I have tried to help you understand your faults,
The ways in which you destroy your own happiness,
Create your own loneliness —
The way you celebrate isolation,
Yet complain of its emptiness.

It's no secret that you still need to grow,
But I can't be your catalyst anymore.

Our marriage has become
A burial ground
For joy.

Perhaps it is time
Our relationship
Lay down to rest with it.

One day, I'll wake up in a beautiful room well-lit by the sun. It will be 6 a.m. in the morning, and I will roll over in bed for another 15 minutes. In 20 minutes, I will finally peel open my eyelids. I will look next to me and see your face, filling my heart with love. At this time, I will have felt it for a while, and it will be natural to love you. I will embrace you and think to myself, "Thank God." Thank God I walked away from the broken pieces of my dreams when I did; otherwise, I would be crying instead of smiling, feeling empty instead of whole. Thank God I left behind a broken past for a peaceful future. Thank God.

SMOKE

I tell myself you are just a cloud
While I am the shining sun,
But when I hear your voice,
I know without a doubt,
You are nothing less than fire.

I tell myself I won't be burned
By your callous touch and hold.
You'll soon become less than a whisper
As I wish away my love and hope.

I convince myself I can't be scorched,
When you are out of view
But when I wake to a room filled with *smoke*,
There's no denying I was dreaming of you.

I am the woman who walks away in a heartbeat,
No questions asked, no true goodbye.
I am a heartbreak waiting to happen,
A car crash avoided too many times,

I am not the woman you make into a game,
A puzzle that keeps you on your toes.
I am not here to be demoralized,
Nor was I made to feel trivial and small.

I know who I am and all I can be,
But with your touch, comes a wave of uncertainty.
Your tongue tells me a different story,
And I begin to forget my journey.

Your eyes thaw and mesmerize me,
And I soon surrender myself completely
Because for this love,
I will be anyone — *anything* —
*Y*ou want me to be.

- Love is not blind; it is near-sighted

You're my yesterday, today, tomorrow.
You're my thought through every sorrow.
I can't even imagine how hollow
Life would be without your tender kiss.

Without you, I'd be a ghost and you, my shadow.
I would be haunting old homes forever,
Just walking, wailing and waiting
For the day we could be smiling
Once again, in each other's arms.

For the sake of all our memories,
Don't you dare walk away and leave me.
I won't just be devastated,
I will be completely shattered.
I will set the world on fire
And keep it burning until forever
As a symbol of my undying love
And a tribute to the person I once was.

Because without you,
There is no person left in me —
I'm just a ghost of the woman I could have been,
With you.

You said I made you feel at home.
I told you that was nothing new,
For to me, home was always with you.
You kissed my cheek,
We spoke for hours,
Then fell asleep.
Before I knew it,
Morning had arrived.
I peeled open my eyes,
Searched for your smile,
But it was nowhere to be found.
When I woke up the next day,
I searched every inch of our home
But you were gone.

You made my house into a home
And then left me *homeless.*

I am shaken by the horror in these books,
Of letters never sent to you,
Of time spent pondering what I would do
If I never heard another word from you.

And I can't help but wonder if one day,
I'll hear you have a book of horrors too,
Filled with letters never sent
To me, from you.

- When the ego trumps the heart

They called it heartbreak,
But my whole body ached for you when you left.
I didn't cry puddles of tears —
I cried enough to fill rivers
That became a swimming pool
I would dip into
From time to time
When I saw old photos,
That I would sink in to
When the reality that you were gone
Hit me like a tornado,
Shook my world like an earthquake.

They called it heartbreak,
But my tongue stung from the times
I bit it so hard, I tasted blood
To stop myself from telling our story.
My head ached from the screaming,
Chanting, repeating
I pushed myself to do
To force myself to get over you —
He's gone, he doesn't love you;
He's gone, silly girl, move on.

They called it heartbreak,
But despite the pain I felt
In every inch of my body,
It was my legs that ached the most,
Because every step forward without you
Was the worst pain I had ever felt.

There were no last words between us,
Just a lonely silence.

It was the loudest silence I had ever heard.

One shot of tequila,
I feel my sadness settle.
Down two beers,
Nothing else matters.
A shot of whiskey
Will do the trick.
Perhaps it will help me
Feel less sick.
A bottle of wine
And I should be fine,
Until tomorrow.

And when tomorrow comes,
I'll start all over.
I'll do whatever it takes
To drown out my sorrows.

- How to get over you

We could have had everything
Had you been in the relationship
Instead of in your head,
Overthinking your way out of love.

I reach out and take your hands
And we dance in circles
With our bodies and words.
Our lips, they touch;
Our souls, they merge.
The taste of earth and sweet syrup,
Marvelling in courage,
Making love on the floor,
The world ignored.
No interest in what they think
When we are on the brink
Of paradise.

We waltz and we walk
To celebrate our win
On water and gin.
Broken glass and promises —
They are things of the past;
Away they are cast
As we circle and spin,
Ignoring the cuts and the sting
Until we can't take it anymore
And our feet are too store
So we open our eyes
To the truth of white lies
And find we are miles apart
In physicality and heart.

My fists closed in my lap,
Our dreams collapse,
Paradise slips away,
My hips they sway
In my seat.

     …

…
I try to reach out again
But with my eyes open,
My hands don't move
Any closer to hold you.
I guess you were just
A dream come untrue.

- Ghosts

I still look through old photo albums,
Reminisce on old memories,
Painfully relive heartbreak,
Remember better days
When it was you and me
Against the world.
Now it's just me,
Alone and unheard.

When you learn to get over someone
By giving your body to someone else,
Placing your worth
In the hands of a man,
Being inside you, feeling you up,
Although it's supposed to be good for you,
It just hurts.

You smile and pretend you like it,
Act like you're over him,
That it's time for you
To finally fall in love with you.
Independence and liberation —
That's what this meaningless sex is all about.
You give yourself a pep talk
To get yourself through.

But soon it's over and he leaves.
You say goodbye,
Leave a kiss on his cheek
But your suppressed tears
Can't be held back any longer.
You cry, fill up the bathtub with gin —
Let the alcohol clean off that stranger.
Whatever is needed
To mend this broken heart.

They say they start missing you
When you stop missing them,
So maybe that means
I won't hear from you again.

- There is no end to missing you

You said we would hang white curtains in our room
Even though you knew I preferred black.
Never you mind –
I've already painted the white curtains in red,
Throwing wine at them while I drink alone at night,
Wrote your name on them and crossed it out twice,
Burned the ends, like you burned our photos.
I've ripped these curtains to pieces,
Destroyed them completely,
But in my room, they hang.

I've done everything else —
Everything else,
But I just can't take these curtains down.

I have spent years now
Screaming at the top of my lungs
In the places I once cried,
Dancing in circles
Around the places my spirit once died,
Laughing through the pain,
Smiling through the sorrow,
Pounding at the concrete ground
To finally see some colour.

I have swallowed my tears,
Starved your demons,
Confronted my fears,
Killed the brain cells
That embody your essence
With tequila and absinth.
I have silenced the voices
That whisper your name,
Drowned them out
With rum and gin.

I have stood still in tornados
And embraced cold winds,
Screamed into velvet pillows
That felt like your skin.

I have done all I can
To escape your shadow,
Yet despite how far I go,
Your memories still follow.

- You are inescapable

These late-night cravings
Cannot be satisfied
Without tasting you
Just one last time.

- Let me taste the sugar on your lips

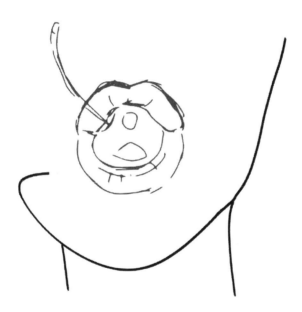

When you left me high and dry,
I decided to be better,
Instead of begging you to stay,
Instead of staying bitter.
I took all the love I had for you
And poured it into a glass.
I mixed it with fine wine and lime
And drank it with my dinner.

I scrubbed your stain right off my skin
With water, soap, and lavender.
I cut the length right off my hair
And tossed it in the fire.
I spent each day treating myself
To warm tea, bubble baths, and candles.
I sang myself sweet songs of love
And smiled at the woman in the mirror.

I felt renewed as I bettered myself.
With a new look and new thoughts,
I transformed into someone else,
But with all that changed,
What never did
Was my hope that you would notice.

So maybe all along I was doing this for you
And despite my efforts to deceive myself,
Even self-love was loving you...

I know that it's hard,
But I wish it wouldn't be
When I'm waiting for you,
Staring at the ceiling;
The ceiling fan spinning,
While I wait for it to fall,
Throwing whiskey rocks at it
While waiting for you to call.

Do you remember the sunflowers
In the park we laid in,
How every passer-by watched
As we smiled and blushed?

Do you remember the feeling
Of kissing in a stairwell,
The sparks that flew so freely
They hit everyone in proximity?
Even when we tried,
We couldn't hide the chemistry.

Do you remember what it was like
To hold hands that one last time,
The day you told me you would miss me
Before you walked away and left me?

Do you remember the feeling
Of knowing what we had was love,
Being in the moment with me,
Letting yourself feel,
Nothing more,
Nothing less,
Just being ourselves?

Do you remember?

Because I can't forget.

Maybe he felt vulnerable
Because he finally had something to lose
And so, he went and destroyed it himself.

- *Self-sabotage*

Thinking of you comes easily; it's automatic.
I waste minutes, hours, and days doing it.
I remember all the beautiful moments we shared —
The feeling of your lips touching mine,
Your silk skin brushing against my legs,
Our hands and souls intertwined,
Gently making our way through life —
But the nostalgia quickly turns to pain
As I remember the heartbreak that always followed,
As if it were a suitcase we dragged along with us
Everywhere we went
Until its weight eventually became too much
And we had no choice left
But to unpack.

- Baggage

Will I ever be free
Of the chains that hold me down,
The ropes that tie me
To this past I still live in with you
But *alone?*

What would you think if you read these letters?
Would you feel guilty
If you read the sweet memories I have of you?
Maybe this is the problem.
I paint you in such a flattering light
When at times, your edges were nothing but sharp.
They cut me in numerous places,
Spilling blood and leaving scars,
But I dared not complain
Because I found comfort in the pain
That was caused by you.

- It was all I had left

What if I'm addicted to the pain
Because it's all I've ever felt,
And I can't let go of our fights
Because they're the only passion left?

You were a spark,
I was a flame.
We travelled lifetimes
Through our embrace,
But when we came back
From distant travels,
We found the world we left behind
Burned to shambles.

You were a spark,
I was a flame,
But together,
We were volatile,
No less rampant
Than a wildfire,
Destroying everything
That came within a mile
Of our love.

Do you get it, the reason I feel the way I do?
I don't, but I was hoping you would.
Somewhere in the chaos of life
You may be contemplating too:
What comes next? What do you do?
Stay where you are both in loneliness and in company
Or adventure further and possibly find me?
Don't go there, my dear,
We both know how it ends.
It ends in circles
Like a fairy-tale starting all over again.
No happily ever after,
Just on repeat like before.
Still, I think of you sometimes
When I eat your favourite meal
Or lay alone on a cold floor.

The tears don't fall anymore
But although the rain has stopped,
The rainbow hasn't come either.
If it did, it would be only two colours —
The brown of your eyes
And blue like the ice in your heart —
The heart that still remains with me
By the way,
When do you want it back?
It's been sitting here all dusty,
Wasting away from all the cracks.
I tried to plaster it together
But I think I made it worse
Because I filled all the empty spaces
With all my empty words.

...

...

Take it back some time and give it to her:
The girl who you lie naked in bed with,
Wondering, *where did love go*?
When you should be enjoying your time,

You send me photographs instead,
Of you and her naked,

Making the love we may or may not have had.
It's kind of fucked up, but I find it poetic.
Even when we're apart, it's like we can't be,
Maybe in distance and physicality,
But not mentally or emotionally
Because you're still thinking of me,
Thinking of our memories:
Us dancing at a cottage

Or in the shower of a hotel room,
Or the day you told me

You never wanted anything more.
Neither did I, until I realized there was more,

More than white lies, confusion, and hurt.

You had asked why I stayed

When I knew someday, I'd have to leave.
I stayed so that I could leave
With a few more bittersweet memories
Of the way you looked at me when you laughed

Or how you held me when I was cold,
Of how I would scream out in rage
And you would sit there staring at me
With that mediocre look in your eyes
That said you'd be patient —
You'd let me speak and then hug me later.

Or how you'd storm out the door and slam it so hard,
It felt like I was slipping through the cracks in the floors.

...

You didn't open it again; that was the last time.
I can still remember the look in your eyes:
Pain and loss, confusion, despair.
Just know, darling,
I never wanted to take you there.
It's why I finally left
With nothing but a tear
And your heart inevitably in my hands.
When do you want it back, by the way?
You know, *it's still here.*

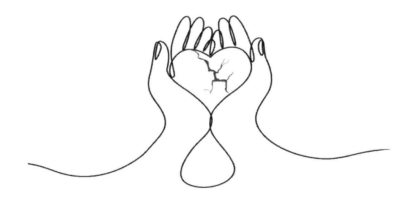

The hardest part is not knowing
Whether I am in love with you
Or the idea of you,

And I can't bet my entire life
On an idea.

- Limitations

What is meant for you
Will not pass you,
But perhaps you can pass
What is meant for you.

- The downside of free will

Someone once told me
That the most passionate lovers
To have ever existed
Are night and day.

Selflessly,
They have spent eternity
Chasing one another
In endless circles,
Pledging their lives
To continue searching
For their lovers.

But only when one
Lays down to rest,
Does the other appear.
Despite their tireless attempts,
Night and day do not meet.

It is beautiful but tragic
To waste one's life
Striving to change the inevitable,
Chasing the unattainable.
It reminds me of us —
How even love
Was not enough
To keep us together.

Perhaps it is time we accept
That like night and day,
We too are destined
To leave our love story
Incomplete.

- *Perhaps we are better apart*

I love you like a Sunday,
A wonderful day of rest,
A sweet escape from reality,
Pancakes in the morning,
Snuggles in front of the TV,
A romantic comedy on the screen.

I love you like a Sunday,
The day before the tragedy
Of waking and working
Until we are aching and pouring
All that we have
Into a glass
For others to sip from.
Sacrificing our lives,
Day by day
And far too fast.

I love you like Sunday,
Like the calm before the storm,
And although Sundays are beautiful
— A lovely dream, a sweet escape —
They are nothing more
Than a break
Before reality
Comes crashing through our doors.

I love you like a Sunday,
But there are six other days in a week.

If the right thing feels wrong,
Is it really the right thing?

- Guilt

You know what's funny about hearts?
When they break, they shatter
Like glass
Into hundreds of little pieces. '
They sit waiting
For someone to piece them
Together,
Like a puzzle.
Who on this earth dares
Piece this broken heart
Back together?

But when someone offers that heart tools —
A hammer, nails, some glue,
Cheers her on,
Tells her she can do the hard work
Of healing on her own,
She cannot help but refuse.

Suddenly, that heart prefers
All her pieces be left unmoved.

- Shattered is comfortable.
		Healing is hard work

FIRE

I am not an open book -
Somewhere on these pages
Are hidden words
That I no longer read,
Dare not speak.
They are fantasies,
Old memories
That surface only in my dreams.

I am not an open book, you see,
There are secrets that hide
Within my spine.
These pages are my very own

Diary.

They say a graveyard is where you rest —
Alone, buried in the soil, nature eating your flesh.
But the graveyard I see is but a dream
Where those who leave this hell walk free.

- The graveyard is where you *wake*

She ran through life like it was a race,
Succeeded at every step,
Overcame every obstacle she faced.
She moved mountains in pursuit of her goals.
But when she finally reached the finish line,
She did not feel relieved,
Nor did she feel successful.
There was a pit in her stomach.
She finally felt the grief
That was eating away at her heart
For far too long.
The speed at which she ran
Was a double-edged sword.
She had everything she always wanted,
Yet nothing that mattered.

- What is success *really*?

Blue for the calm before the storm,
Green for the colour of grass that doesn't grow.
Orange for the sight of fall leaves falling
Until there are no trees left growing.
Pink for the young girls forced to model,
Fuchsia for those that are still just toddlers.
Grey is the sound of crying daughters,
Remembering home and missing their mothers.
Red for the wails of hurting women,
Stuck in homes they don't want to live in.
Black for the sound of a firing pistol,
When women can't find help in a broken system.
Brown for the colour of broken trust.
Plum for the feeling of wasted love,
Your body deciding to give in to lust.
Pine for the feeling of being called a 'slut'.
White for innocence that's slowly leaving.
Hazel for weary eyes tired of weeping.
And when nothing else can support your healing,
Silver for the knife that ends your grieving —
At least for a moment.

- The modern rainbow

There is no way to grow within or break through
These systems that are built on patriarchy,
When their very foundation is women's oppression.

- We must build from the ground up

At first glance
These buildings appear clean,
Neat and tidy.
But beneath the rugs and wood,
The place is filthy —
Rich with history
Of abuse and horror,
Of weeping children,
Devastated mothers,
And historical sorrows.

In the cold, stone walls
Are bones and blood
Giving the buildings
A chilling touch.
This history of misery
Should have been a push
Towards remorse and reflection
Growth and repentance.
But instead of owning up
To mistakes of the past,
They maintain the façade
Of living faultless and devout.

They profess their love
For sinners and neighbours
As they find new ways
To excuse their behaviours.
They worship a God
With hope and heart
To help them turn the page
To a fresher start.
          …

...

Without admittance of wrongs,
They sing devotional songs,
Yet put on white gloves
To hide the blood
That has hardened
On their *holy hands*.

We live in a society
Where members silence their opinions
To desperately hide themselves;
Where those who speak their minds
Are seen as insensitive, incorrect,
And are brutally attacked;
Where the majority of the population
Jumps on a bandwagon
In an attempt to feel validated,
Without realizing
That absorbing societal opinions
Is only violating
To their own sense of self.
This desperate attempt to feel valued
Leads to a lack of what is desired,
As there is no value at all
In not thinking for yourself.

- Please tell me,
What is the problem with forming your own opinions?

Why do we insist on wasting our words
When they are powerful enough
To destroy cities, empty rivers, create wars;
When they can cause heartbreak, excessive pain,
False happiness, memories that last lifetimes,
And regrets that last just as long?
Why do we throw around
Meaningful words like, *I love you,*
When what we truly mean is, *I don't want to be alone?*
Why do we tell people we want to be with them forever
When what we mean is 'forever' *for now?*
How do we drown out that uncomfortable feeling within us
When we know we are deceiving
But don't want to admit it aloud.

- Your words are your currency; spend them well

What is it about these holy books
That creates unnecessary segregation?
Everyone thinks their beliefs are truth,
But is that not just ignorance?
Everyone believes their God is the only God,
But if there is 'one God',
Are not all Gods the same?

And to those that frown at people
Who believe in more than one deity —
What is our evidence that these deities
Are not what we believe in,
Yet see as one?

Believing that our Gods
— Whether there are one, two or five —
Are different in any way
Is a belief limited to the human mind.
A number coined by humans
And the characteristics they assign,
Do not mean these Gods are any different
Than the one worshipped by you or I.

- Your God is my God

You cannot wrap your head around the concept
That you are all using different words
To preach the same faith,
But I cannot wrap my mind around
The limited belief systems
That suggest we are not all the same humans,
Bleeding the same blood,
Desiring similar desires, and
Falling victim to the same human fate.

I am told I have a problem,
With not letting things go.
When you lied to me,
I was attentive,
And the lies turned into a snowball
Of little things that made no sense,
Of absurd possibilities,
All of which seemed
Unbelievable to me.

I am told that I obsess
Over irrelevant facts
Like the sound of his voice
When he said goodbye
Or the letters she wrote
And eventually threw away,
Whether it was sunny and warm
Or raining on a given day.

I am told that I interrogate
Asking questions
With no end in sight,
That I ask for details
No one will remember
All to get a clear answer,
That my focus is too large —
But even your focused camera
Couldn't capture all these scars.

When you're told that you're crazy
Or mentally unwell,
You start to believe it, feel it,
Act like you are.
            …

...
I started taking medication
To limit my thoughts
To less than fifty a day.
When the facts didn't make sense,
I drank my thoughts away.

But now I can see
That I was never crazy;
In fact, I was wise,
Smarter than many,
More dedicated than most
To resolving the issues
And discovering the truth.

The fact that I could interrogate,
Ask for details,
Challenge what didn't make sense,
Tells me I did exactly the opposite
Of what my abuser had expected.
More questions meant more lies
But those lies got me closer
To learning the truth
Because at a certain point,
Nothing fit together;
The story line didn't make sense.

So maybe I was traumatized in the process,
Maybe my approach was a weakness,
But the obsession was my strength,
Because without it,
I would never have ended my abuse.

- *Survivor*

You broke me,
Shattered my hopes and dreams,
Yet have the audacity to ask
Why I am missing pieces.

I learned to be whole with what I had left

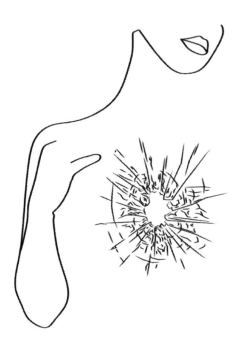

I peeled my layers, one by one —
I made myself vulnerable,
So I could finally share with you my pain
And in response to hearing my tragedy,
You asked me
Why I went searching for it.

- Victim-blaming

You hit rock bottom,
Shattered all your bones
While I stood tall at the top,
Looking down at you.
When your gaze met mine,
Your face went white,
And I knew you had finally realized
I would not be joining you this time.

- I will not let you drag me down with you anymore

As she puts you on a pedestal
And ignores the nagging feeling in her gut
Because of the tugging at her heart,
As she silences the alarm bells
That are calling out her name
To warn her,
I cry for her.

- The hardest part of leaving
        is knowing someone else
                will take your place

Your words are beautiful —
They tell stories I can get lost in for hours.
You speak of all things in life that matter:
Love,
Hope,
Peace,
Truth,
Integrity.
But although your words are captivating,
Words are all they will ever be
If you do not act.
You can tell me you love me all you want;
You can tell me that I am 'the one'
But none of that means anything
Unless you find a way to *show me.*

I don't fall in love with words; *I fall in love with people*

It is soul shattering to admit
That I spent years
Waiting for this moment to come
And now that it's finally here,
I no longer see the man I love;
Instead, I see an old memory,

And I cannot marry a ghost.

I wish you were here,
So I could tell you how loneliness
Has been a better friend to me
Than you ever were.

- Thank you for leaving

Time may pass,
But I will move with it.

What's it like when you're with her?

Do you feel young like you did with me, or old like a man who lost his youth in the time spent working instead of kissing?

Do you feel butterflies in your stomach, or the hurricane you felt when I told you I was leaving?

Do you feel like jumping up and down when she calls your name, or was that feeling reserved for someone you were unwilling to believe in?

Do her cries create a pit in your stomach that even your sweetest, most sincere apologies can't undo?

Does she make you feel like destiny is a thing and God real, or does it make your faith shake when you realize she is not me, *or* have you given up on the God we talked about already?

Do you love her dearly, or do you convince yourself that love is bland, like the piece of toast you eat at night when instead you could be tasting me?

What's it like when you're with her?

Is it anything close to how it was when you were with me?

Tell me.

It was a blessing in disguise
That you did not leave enough breadcrumbs

For me to find my way home to you,
That you dropped only the number
Needed to confuse me and keep me on my toes,
That it backfired when I lost my way
And was forced to build a new home for myself

With higher gates and clearer boundaries,
That I finally realized I didn't need your crumbs
When I could make myself
A whole damn feast.

Thank you for the memories
Of your smile,
Of your laugh,
Of breaking my heart,
Playing games, showing care,
Withdrawing out of nowhere,
Promising me forever,
Changing feelings like the weather,
Showering me with love,
Turning pennies into diamonds,
Gold into steel,
Speaking words without meaning,
Having me believing,
Kissing in the rain,
Trading love in for fame,
Playing me like a violin,
Breaking all my strings,
Calming me with your voice,
Saying you'd made your choice,
Giving no explanation,
Adding to my frustration,
Saying our last goodbyes,
Watching me cry,
Coming back to say hello,
Not letting me go,
Claiming you'd always love me,
Throwing away the only key
To my heart.

- *Thank you*

Because when all is said and done,
I need someone who sees that problems are temporary,
But that love is *permanent.*

When it rains, it pours.
The rain used to be warm
And it smelled like you.
It felt like your roses and thorns.
Now, it's cold and filled with pain.
It tries to wash sins away
But washes away sinners.
The rain decided
They wouldn't get any cleaner.

When it rains, it pours
Bloody showers.

They say you can't love two people,
But then, why do I feel the way I do?
I love you more than you can imagine
But still, I think of him when I'm with you —
His fragrance, those eyes, his beautiful smile,
Our effortless embrace —
All I want to do is run
My fingers down his face.

When I'm with him, it feels good
Until I think of you.
It is not difficult to see
That what I feel is true.
I think of your soft lips
Kissing my cheeks,
And although my legs are strong,
My knees go weak.

They say you can't love two people,
So I must have broken the rules.
Although it's been hard to admit,
I take pride in speaking the truth.
There is no falseness to my feelings,
But society wants me to feel shame.
I used to pray my memories of love
Would eventually fade,
But it has been years and years
And the feelings have stayed.

Now that I have made my peace
With how I feel,
I must ask you why
We think in black and white.
It is so damn limiting
When there is so much grey
To try to simplify
The human mind.

I refuse to comply
To these oppressive norms.
You hold falsified standards
To which I will not conform.
We must educate ourselves
On the rules we're conditioned to follow,
And it does take courage,
But my pride I swallow
As I allow myself to fall victim
To misguided wrath —

Rather than acknowledge the problem,
They shoot the messenger instead.

- Still, *I would rather be a dead messenger than a puppet*

Loving two men,
In a strange way,
Helps me feel free.
There are so many intricacies to being human, and
I am finding them in me.

- Loving two is better than loving none

They tell us to live and to love,
Not to lust, not to fuck.
Our bodies are the temples
They try to take from us.

- Control

You can try as hard as you want to shove me into your carefully constructed boxes of prejudice, but I promise you that, despite your best efforts to fit me neatly into the confines of those four walls, *I will not fit.*

Your boxes are far too small for me.

You say I need oversight,
But why would I need your insights,
Your guidance and review
Over the things that I do?
The words that I speak
Are mine alone to keep.
And I will choose what is edited,
Altered, or removed.

How unauthentic it would be
For me to claim words as my own
When, like those of the rest of the world,
They have been *censored*.

When they put words in your mouth,
Remember to spit them out.

- *You speak for yourself*

HELLFIRE

I am not here to put out your fires;
I am here to ignite them.

Her intelligence and strength
Make you feel emasculated and small,
So you push her to the ground
And watch her crawl.
You must expect her life to stop
When you try to take her place
And make your way to the top.

But listen darling,
You must be forgetting,
No one in the world
Can stop her from growing.
Don't you remember
What they used to say?
Don't underestimate your enemies;
You'll only lose that way.

Say what you will,
Do what you do.
It won't be long before you tire,
Realizing –
You're only adding fuel to *hellfire.*

You once called me a failure,
But I have some news for you.
If failure means losing,
Then yes, I lost my heart to you.
And while you won,
Stealing every part of me you could —
You stripped me naked,
You didn't rest
Until you had
*Even my skin in your hand*s —
I was still standing
And with my legs shaking,
I walked away.
So if failure means losing,
Well, *you lost me.*

Do not underestimate a woman with burns on her torso
From the fire raging in her belly,
Scars on her heart and hands
From pouring endless love and mending broken men,
And eyes that look nowhere but ahead —

It is your disbelief that fuels her strength.

Unanticipated and abrupt,
The blinds of my eyes opened up.
Feelings of rage overcame the sadness stored away,
Anger at the hurting I didn't deserve to experience,
Memories of running out of tears, time, years.
All the times I cried, screamed,
And slammed my fists against a dry wall,
The times I couldn't walk, I had to crawl.
When hate of this world overpowered my will to live,
An empty heart is what I had to live with.
I let myself be defeated, feel defeated, feel small,
But no longer will I let my power be taken.
Today, I'm rising, standing tall,
Picking up my crown.
It had fallen to the ground,
When I lowered my head in shame.
You had tried to put in on,
But on you, it was too small —

This crown was always meant for a queen.

She did not dance with the devil;
The devil danced with her.

They would tell me to calm down
As if their words would make a difference
To the fire raging inside me
From the lies, abuse, and fear
I constantly choked on.

They would tell me to let it go
As if you can unlearn
Every piece of information
You fought nearly to the death for.

The truth doesn't come easily
In a world of deceit;
I paid heavily for every bit of it,
The price being my own inner peace.

They placed me on a foundation of sticks,
On which I could barely find balance,
Convinced me to suppress my anger
And replace it with love and compassion.
But every generous piece of advice they gave me,
Was nothing but a feeble attempt
To support their own selfish desires.

Still, they tell me to let it go —
Don't they know?
When hanging off the edge of a cliff,
Letting go is not an option
For someone who has made a habit of surviving.

- *I won't let it go.*

It's the way you quench your thirst with wine
While saying you need water,
When what you really need
Is an ocean filled with tears
To show you just how much
You've made others cry.

You attended to my bruises,
Put Band-Aids on the wounds
That needed stitches, love, and healing,
But Band-Aids don't erase feelings.
Still, you somehow have the audacity to ask
How the cuts you made left a scar.

There is no magic wand to wave;
Healing takes time.

It has felt like *emptiness*
Since you said her name,
Like the sunshine we once bathed in
Is covered by grey clouds.
Even when they move,
The sun refuses to shine through.

I used to feel like myself,
Happy and free,
But you took that away,
Made me feel uncomfortable
In my own skin
To the point where I had to peel it all off,
Let my body bleed for a while,
Then grow it back,
New and fresh.

You fucked with my mind,
Played games with it,
Stepped on my heart
Because of insecurity?
Clearly,
You were not deserving of me —
But I hold the winning cards now.

You ask me to stay,
But it's like she's in between us
When we're fucking
And I just can't fucking
Let that go.

- Consequences

If I can't be your number one,
I'll be your nothing-at-all.

- Standards

You were 'the one' —
The only one,
Until you made promises
You could not keep,
Told me we would grow old together
Before I watched you leave.
You used to be 'the one'
But now, you're just *one of the rest.*

- How you became *unspecial*

There was a time
When I would have clawed my heart out of my chest
And given it to you in your hands,
When I would have walked ten hours, bare foot, to see you
Even if my feet bled

There was a time
When I would have ripped the skin right off my bones
To clothe you,
When I would have set my soul on fire
Just to hold you.

There was a time
When I would have left behind my entire life
To spend one night in your arms,
Given up everything I had ever known
To let you birth a few more scars.

That time has passed.

I write our love story on blank pages
To fill the emptiness in my heart.
The blank look in my eyes
That I am asked about
Stays hidden behind sunglasses
Far too large for me,
But they hide my tears well.
You wouldn't be able to tell
It was me if you saw me.
You changed me.
You've got to know,
When you set my body on fire,
Like a snake,
My skin shed.

I used to be a dull orange
That faded to peach when you left,
Turned to green over time,
Feeling jealous of your new love –
You were mine.
Time passed and I turned blue
Every time I cried for you
And you didn't come.
Now, I am bright red
Because of the zealous rage
I feel in my chest.

I don't cry tears anymore,
I create rivers.
I don't light candles anymore,
I burn bridges.
I burn any that lead back to
Whom I once was.

            …

...
I will never be the same
As when you left
Because that vulnerability
I used to have
Left me shattered,
Missing you.
Now they call me, 'put together',
Only thinking of you
When I write these words called poems
To keep forgetting you exist.
The irony kills me,
But as I've said,
I'm different now
So I stay alive.

Our story ended a long time ago,
Yet I go over it in my mind every day.
Maybe you will come back one day
And I will finally tell it to you.
Maybe the story of how you made me feel
Will make you shake.
Maybe it will fill you with guilt
And you will try to make it up to me,
Pretend to love me.
Maybe I'll let you
Until I get back at you
By walking away.
I'll take back the power
You once took away from me
When you begin to hope we last longer.
Maybe I'll shock you
Because you thought I couldn't live without you,
But I'll leave you nonetheless
After leaving a sweet kiss on your neck —
Lipstick, stained red.
You can leave it on forever,
Hang my picture in front of your mirror
So that you can see us together —
You can see me looking back,
While knowing deep in your heart
That you will never have me back.

- I guess you shouldn't have left in the first place

Maybe it was a picture I painted in my head,
Maybe it was an obsession.
Maybe everything I felt was entirely correct,
Maybe it was imagination.
Maybe it was fact
Like how even in the darkest of nights,
Your eyes still shine like day —
But then again,
Maybe it was just an opinion,

And opinions can change.

When I see two lovers part
And the man breaks his woman's heart
Out of fear of adventure
And passion that could light fires
For a mediocre life that is safe,
For a woman that is tame —
I remember how you left
What was meant to be
For something forced and empty.
I still remember the sound
Of your footsteps walking away
From the best thing that ever happened to you —
Me.

My future never looked brighter,
And your past never looked better.

- Breakups

I can picture you sitting at a well-crafted marble table at seventy, pouring overpriced whiskey into a glass and drinking away no longer existent worries, which worries you even more. You'll look around your oversized dream house and wonder where in it you got lost, when you traded me in for it. You will think of me then. Wherever you are in your life, you will think back – your thoughts feeling like a time machine – and remember me. And if you do not feel it now, you will feel your regret then. I can only hope the alcohol kicks in quickly enough to numb your aching heart. You'll wish my love was with you then, but it won't be. *You lost me.*

Just remember —
You're not the one that got away;
You're the one that left,
And there isn't any comfort for you in that.

I am not the heartache I felt
But the strength that came after.
I am not the pain I endured
But the laughter that came later.
I am not the frustration I felt
But the calm that washed over me.
I am not the resentment I held
But the peace that flows through me.

I am not the negativity
That has worn out its welcome in my life.
I am not defined by a careless man
Who breaks hearts in the blink of an eye.
I am not the stupidity I felt
When I was young and trusting.
I am not the silence
I once found disturbing.
I am not a commodity
To be used when it is convenient and fun.

Lastly,
I am not an item on your bookshelf;
I am the fire you can't sell.
You can't put a price tag on me
Or rub me down like I'm a trophy.
I am not the little girl you see in me;
I am the woman I fought to be,
And *this woman isn't yours.*

Can you hear my silent screams of success?
It has taken me time to accept
That I am better than I gave myself credit for
Because I went through the hardest times all alone
And still came out better;
I still came out stronger.

- Yes, you can keep calling me 'put together.'
I haven't fallen apart just yet

You will search for me
In every woman you meet,
In every relationship you see.
You will look for the parts of me
You could never truly grasp,
The pieces of my puzzle
You could never fit together.

Over and over again,
You will listen to others' stories
And compare them with our own,
In hopes of finally understanding
Where two people
Who were once so right together
Went so wrong.

Years later,
When you finally meet the right woman,
You will forget me for one moment
When you look into her eyes,
But the second a moment passes,
You will look down at her smile
Expecting to see mine.

When she kisses your lips
You will crave the sugar you tasted on my tongue.
When you feel the warmth of her embrace,
You will miss the shiver I sent down your spine.
You will look up at her face
And search every inch for features
That resemble the ones you caressed in our bed,
Kissed under our sheets.

...

...
That's when it will hit you
That no matter what you do,
What you say,
Where you go,
You cannot outrun the regret of leaving me.
You cannot escape the demons
That wear my face.

Forever and always, we said.
This is how I keep my promise.

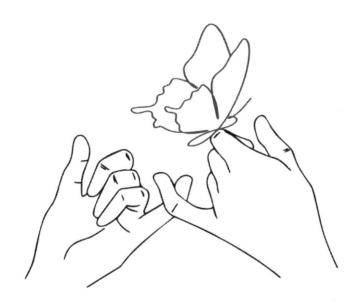

I am not your damsel in distress,
I am free.
I own the distress,
It does not own me.
I live above the skies
In a world of my own making.
I am not your damsel in distress
In need of saving.

I will not drown in deep rivers,
But walk on their waters.
I will not burn in fires,
I will tame them.
Even the fear you feel
Is afraid of me.
I am not your reward,
You cannot afford me.

Your guns and knives,
Your violent tries
Will not do.
I have my own weapons —
My heart,
My brain,
My truth.
I have the blood of strong women
Flowing through my veins
So no, despite your tries,
I am not here to be enslaved.

...

...

I am not your damsel in distress,
I do not need saving.
Your free help and cheap lies,
The superiority you hide inside,
Your calculated smiles are costly.
I will not fall victim to the patriarchy
You so willingly embody

I am not your damsel in distress.
I am a survivor, nothing less.
I have been fighting off monsters
My entire life
So trust me when I say,
They look a lot like you.

They say, *don't let your intensity show.*
I say, *don't listen to them,*
Don't let your intensity go.
You speak your mind
And some people mind
As if your words, your truths
Cause them personal pain.

It's time to tame
The lioness, they say,
Your intensity only scares people away.
When you open your mouth,
They cower and shake.
It's not that you intend to hurt,
Intend to break.

Your words are just words,
Words they think of as weapons
But that you know
Are only just a reflection
Of the truest truths,
Your deepest desires,
And sometimes those truths
Happen to set fires.

They say, *let your intensity go.*
I say, *why won't you let your intensity show?*
Life is short and you're wasting away,
Leaving behind your yesterdays —
Your words unspoken, your heart unopened.
What's the point of living
If you are living in silence?

They told me to bite my tongue,
But I bit so hard, I tasted blood.

I decided that from then on,
I would always speak my mind.

When you put her down,
She laughs at your words,
Knowing very well
That she's the snake and you're the bird.
Calm and calculated,
She'll slither and hiss,
Choosing to bite
When there's no chance of a miss.
A golden poison
Flowing through your blood,
Killing you slowly —
An antidote
No one else knows of.
So you'll rely on her forgiveness
And apologize,
Realizing that messing with a snake
Wasn't very wise.

You threw me to the wolves,
Thinking I would be devoured.
How silly you were.

You cannot outsmart a woman
Raised in the proximity
Of intergenerational trauma,
Suicide attempts,
Mental illness,
And lifelessness.
The life in her
Is what she fought for
Every day.

You cannot throw a fighter to the wolves
And expect that she be devoured.
She will turn the lost pack into a family,
And make her way back
Leading her captors.

It took me time to reach a place
Of numbness and a lack of care.
I have reached the point
Where I can walk away
From love, family, and friendships
In a heartbeat
If I do not receive
The loyalty I deserve,
The effort required to foster a friendship.
There is no point in allowing
People I once called friends
To take up space in my mind and heart
When they walked into it tracking mud
And left nothing but a pile of ashes
Where there were once flowers.
There is no room for people
Who do not know the first thing about being loyal,
Yet expect it in return.

The difference is that I am busy chasing my dreams
While you are still chasing your demons.

Fear was a faceless monster
That consumed me,
Ate away at my soul,
Swallowed my mind whole.
Rational thinking was a rarity
As I waited for someone to save me,
Feeling like I was again a child
Afraid of the dark,
Screaming for her mother
To come and comfort her.

Fear would tug at my legs
While I tried to sleep.
It would tug at my gut
When I tried to trust.
It would worm its way into my heart
Any time anyone got too close.

Fear was almost the death of me
And I do not say this lightly —
Perhaps I would not be here
Writing these words
If it were not for me.

Because when I realized
That despite what might happen,
However twisted and horrible,
Whether I was happy or miserable,
I would be present at the end of the day
Holding my own hands,
Thrusting myself forward,
Loving the woman in the mirror —
It was a game changer.

      …

...

Fear was no longer faceless.
I saw her face for the first time
And this time,
It was she who was terrified.

Fear consumed me until I said *enough*
        And, in turn, *consumed my fear.*

When I feel weak,
I think of my grandmother,
Of how she worked long hours in a factory
Even after my sister and I were born,
Of how she would still smile
At the end of a hard day
When her body ached
And exhaustion consumed her.

My grandmother did not work herself to the bone
For me to sit around and feel sorry for myself.
She overcame endless obstacles
To give my family and I a better life
Than the one she had been given,
To show us a world more beautiful,
Than the one she had been born into.

When I feel weak,
I think of my grandmother.
I remember my promise to not let her down,
To not let her hard work go to waste.
I pick myself up and stand tall
Because I know that one day,
I'll be strong like her.

My grandmother may have passed
But the strength of her spirit remains with me.

Through the darkest of nights
You were the only star that would shine for me
When my candle died.

You have always been my light.

- Letters to myself

When I look in the mirror, I see brown —
The colour of skin we are told is not beautiful,
The 'exotic' face that is a commodity
To large hands that appear clean but are filthy
With thoughts that label us women as inferior,
That dehumanize us and turn us into objects
To be held, admired, and then disposed of.

When I look in the mirror, I see brown —
The colour of sweat and tears,
The stain of dark, tiring years
Tainted by segregation, oppression, and racism
That I carry on tired shoulders
Like a backpack filled with rocks
That I am told to unpack but can't
Because this burden is an heirloom
That has been passed down through generations.

How can I let go when the history of this burden
Shows strength, resilience, and perseverance?
I will not unpack the backpack of my ancestors
Which gives my weak shoulders character.
I will continue carrying it
And with time and pressure,
The rocks will turn into diamonds
That my great grandchildren will proudly wear.

So when I look in the mirror, I see brown —
The colour of soil that nourishes the natural world,
In which seeds are planted
And strong women like us
Continue to grow.

- *Brown skin*

Water may quench your thirst for a while,
But eventually,
Everyone is drawn to the flame.

RAIN

There is nothing in this world like new beginnings,
And they happen every day.

My heart beats fast for you
But I slow that naïve girl down.
My body aches for you
But I find a way to un-feel your touch.
My lips hum a sweet lullaby
That sounds like your name
And although I love the sound,
I threaten to set my tongue aflame.
My hands try to find you
So I dig my nails deep.
I scream confessions of love;
I have no secrets to keep.
When I dig deeper,
I scream out in pain.
My heart tells me I want you
But I've been told,
This desire
Is just *passing rain.*

Now, I see that the heartbreak
Was only growing pains.

They say home is where the heart is.
My heart had always been with you,
But in a home so big,
I lost myself loving you.

They say home is where the heart is.
My heart had always been with you,
So thank you for finally returning it.
The best thing you ever did for me was leave,
Because when you did,
All that I was left with was me,

And I found a home in her too.

The way I see it,
Every step backwards
Is still a step closer
To whom I am becoming,

And I cannot wait to meet her.

My hope for you
Is that every lie you tell
Is yet another brick in your backpack
Which is already far too heavy
To carry through life.

I do not wish for you to be crushed
By the weight of fabrication and deceit
But instead, hope that what you are carrying
Becomes painful, torturous, and unbearable
To continue moving with
So that you must eventually
Put the backpack down.

My hope for you
Is that life ultimately persuades you
To free yourself with the truth.

It took me time to reach a point
Where I did not hate him,
To reach a place
From which I could approach him
With love and support,
Compassion and understanding.
It took me longer, however,
To realize that if I could forgive him,
I owed myself the same respect.

- How my life changed

You are the villain in your story.

Until you realize this,
You will sabotage your own happiness
By concerning yourself with others,
Thinking they are out to get you,
Entertaining paranoia,
When the truth is
You are the only one
That is holding you back.

I used to be the villain in my story.
Now, I'm my own hero.

Flowers grew in my comfort zone,
But the world waited outside of it.

A voice enters my mind.
It's a different voice; it's not mine.
It is both soft and harsh,
Stern but forgiving,
Demanding but understanding.
Most importantly,
It is convincing,
And I begin to think
These are the best of times
Because when you are lost,
There is so much left to find.

- Lost and found

It is during times like these that you choose
Whether you want to be defined
By failures that are not only yours,
By heartache that shouldn't be yours,
By old, shattered dreams
And worn-out memories,
Or whether you would rather
Be defined by your essence,
The beautiful energy inside of you,
By who you are
Rather than what has happened to you.
It is during times like these
That the one to 'define' you
Is finally you.

The truth is,
You will never be who you were before the trauma,
But you can sure as hell grow from it.

- Even dead flowers can bloom again

Let your shattered heart transform into artwork,
Into a mosaic — unique, and beautiful.
But remember,
The most spectacular pieces of art take time,
Much like healing.

You are the beginning of a masterpiece

I used to hide from my shadows,
Dismiss their existence,
Swallow my feelings whole.
I would run for hours and hours
That turned into days and then months
To get away from anything
That brought me down.

I ended up lost, in a faraway place —
No family, no friends, no love.
I was removed from the world
With nothing and no one to turn to —
Exhausted, isolated, and cold.

When I was too tired to run any further
And I sat down to dwell on my sorrow,
My shadows came creeping in.
They sat down next to me
And kept me company while I cried.
That night, I looked my shadows
Dead in the eye for the first time
And suddenly, I was a little less lonely.

I used to hide from my shadows.
Now, I dance with them in the dark.

We are not who we say we are.
There is no way we can summarize
The complexities of humankind
In a few simple words
And use them to define ourselves.
We cannot be confined
By the limitations of language,
Imprisoned
By expectations and judgments
Translated
Into descriptions of us.
We are not who we say we are;
Our complexity cannot be captured by words.

It is like you are trapped in a dark room
With no sense of peace,
Just a lonely silence,
Yet somehow, somewhere
In the wall of your prison,
There's a crack
From which sunlight, suddenly
Comes pouring in.

You see a rainbow in the sky,
Let out a sigh,
And in the blink of an eye,
Your skin starts peeling,
A thicker layer growing
And you recognize this miracle
Is God speaking.

Somehow your prayers were heard.
No one said a word
But when you look around now,
You see sun and flowers,
Rains and showers
And you wonder why
You ever doubted his promises.

- Miracles

I now thank God
For every barrier, failure, and rejection.
What a waste it would be
To spend time dwelling on roads that are closed
When there are finer paths to walk along
With fresher air and enthralling sceneries.

ASHES

The grass is always greener on the other side —
Until you look closer and see the weeds.

- *Appreciate what you have*

What I feel for you is no longer a mad, passionate, extraordinary love. It just is. It comes with being, with breathing, with living. It is inescapable and unwavering. I am not obsessed, but I think of you every day. I am not irrational, but sometimes I feel you next to me. I do not hallucinate, but sometimes I hear your voice saying my name, tenderly and with love. You are always with me because you reside within me. You always will.

- To the ones we've lost

We all die some day
But knowing this doesn't take the pain away.
It does not make
Losing you any easier.
Instead, I fear
That you have turned into nothingness
So we will never meet again,
Not even at life's end.
They tell me to have faith,
But faith does not take away the bitter taste
Of you being gone.
Faith does not make this broken heart
Feel any better.
It does not put the pieces you left me in
Back together.

- I miss you

I have cried every day since you left.
Even if my eyes are dry,
My heart is wet.
I turn the tears into prayers,
But the pain lives on in my chest.

- RIP

The wind speaks to me in your voice,
The sun shines on me with your grace,
The thunder scolds me with your strength,
The clouds embrace me with your softness,
The rain revitalizes me with your care,
The skies touch me with your love.
You may be in heaven
But I have found you on earth.

You are the calm before the storm,
The waves within the sea.
At night, you are the wind and breeze,
In the morning, my warm cup of tea.

You are the grass growing outside my home,
The fall leaves on the ground.
You are the tree that looks down at fallen fruit,
Yet continues standing tall.

You are the cup of whiskey I smell and sip,
The broken bottles at my feet.
You're the sun I wake to everyday,
The moon that shines down on me as I sleep.

You are the bonfire I can't peel my eyes off,
The smell of burning wood.
You are the steep hill I roll right down,
The valley into which I fall.

You are every shooting star on which
I ever made a wish,
The fairy tale that came to life
When we shared our first kiss.

You are love and longing,
Desire and hope,
The eyes that I adore —
But you're also pain and grieving,
Anger and aching
That I cannot numb or ignore.

...

...

You are everything I see around me,
The good and the bad.
You left and I longed,
Now I sit writing these songs
To keep me company as I bleed.
Yet, at the very least,
I can say that I am at peace
With all your bits and pieces,
Surrounding me.

- You really are my everything

Oh no, darling,
Our love story is not over —
It will live on within these pages.
I will write us into existence once more.
We will have a life together
Even if it is confined to the pages of this book.

- It will be like you never left

Everything is poetry —
The smell of our coffee,
The warmth of our tea.
Everything is poetry —
The fall breeze,
The depths of our seas.
Everything is poetry —
A good book to read,
New places to see.
Everything is poetry,
But y*ou are my muse.*

The grass is green but not green enough.
The sky is blue but it's looking dark.

Our eyes have met but we are worlds apart.
Our love is just a game of hearts.

We come together to be ripped apart.
Who would have thought each end
Would be a fresh start?

The problem is, we are both better off
Without the other in our arms.

But the love we crave cannot be stopped.
Only time will tell
Whether we'll choose our brains or hearts.

So, although I am again saying goodbye,
It is only goodbye until next time.
I'll see you when the day ends in night
And we are drawn to one another
Like a moth to light.

- *We are magnetic*

Even if you don't see the arrow coming,
I will be there to block it,
Said love.

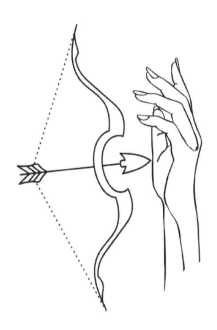

I knew you from before we met —
Your silk skin, a face of porcelain,
The smell of smoke that lingered on your skin,
The feeling of your hold,

The tightening of your chest,

The familiarity of your sweet breath.
I knew you from before we met,
From another world I cannot yet understand.

The earth shakes when I hear your name;
The grey sky turns to gold.
The birds start to sing our favourite song
When we think about growing old,
Sitting together in our beautiful home,
White curtains hanging bold,
Stained with the paint of late-night screams,
A hint of blood on the floor.
My heart can't help but bleed
When you walk out the door.

How the thunder stops and lighting strikes
When you hold me in your arms.
When we want to feel close, yet feel so far
Because no amount of love is ever enough.
My longing and aching never ends;
Your touch truly mends
Every wound I've ever endured,
Most of which were at your hands.

How my knees go weak and my naive heart beats
When you show up in front of me,
Your eyes shining with that glimmer of hope
That I'm hoping, this time, we can keep.
Although the hurt feels like a dagger,
It only makes me stronger —
Strong like we are when we are together.
And still, oh still, you fill me with faith
Because we both know,
This is our fate.

The day we were born,
The skies rained tears of happiness
And cried out in relief.
The dark clouds feasted on one another
Until all that was left was hot sun
To embrace us with loving warmth.
The tall grass danced back and forth
At the command of the wind,
Orchestrating our first dance.

They had all heard
That the universe conspired
To reunite two lost souls
That had been longing for one another
For over a thousand years.
Rolling in their graves,
Calling out each other's names.

The loud wind shushed all the chatter
And whispered our names, one after the other.
Like promises, they appeared on paper.
The day we were born
The birds sang a prophesy;
They told stories of the love
That would exist between you and me.

Since the day we were born,
We were meant to be,
Just two puppets being thrown around
By a force called *destiny*.

From dawn to dusk, I think of you.
From dusk to dawn, I dream of you.

- You do not cross my mind; *you live in it*

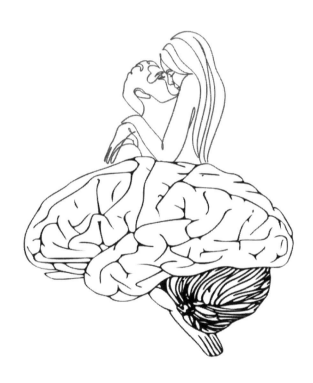

Without love,
We have no lifeboat
To help us sail
Across these stubborn seas.

Without love,
We swim in oceans
Of drowning deaths
And tragedies.

Without love,
We are helpless soldiers
Thrown into lifeless wars
And cruel fates.

- Without love

I have memorized what I will do once I leave.
I have a plan; there is no need to grieve.
When I go, you should know
I'll find peace protecting you.
I will be loving, not losing you.
I will search for happiness and tell it to find you.
You will find peace outside of our memories;
You will finally feel free.
If you cry out in pain, I'll run to your side.
You can picture me holding your hand in mine.
There is nothing more lovely, nothing more true —
I will always be right beside you.

- Even death can't do us apart

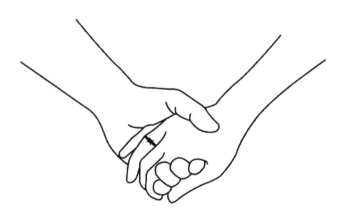

And when this candle dies,
We will light our own flame
And celebrate one another
For a little while longer
Before we inevitably
Reach the point
Where all we can create
Is a fire set by betrayal
And fuelled by hate.

- Let us make the most of right now

Our love is no longer a battlefield.
It is now a playground
For our beautiful children,
And a warm fire
For our souls.

CREDITS

All illustrations in this book, including the cover page, were created by the author on Canva.com, using a range of elements designed by Canva element creators.

Printed in Great Britain
by Amazon

11790879R00127